Contents

Words in **bold** can be found
in the glossary.

The Tudors

The Tudor family ruled England from 1485 until 1603. The Tudor period began when Henry Tudor defeated Richard III at the Battle of Bosworth Field, and was crowned Henry VII.

Tudor rulers

Henry VII was succeeded by his son, Henry VIII, in 1509. Henry's **reign** was one of the most eventful in English history. Not only did Henry marry six times, he also broke away from the **Roman Catholic Church**

and created a new **Protestant** Church of England. The last three rulers of the Tudor period were Henry's three children: Edward, Mary and Elizabeth.

The 45-year reign of Elizabeth I is often known as the 'Golden Age'. Trade and business flourished, as did music, art and literature. Elizabeth did not marry, and the Tudor period came to an end with her death in 1603.

⬅ Queen Elizabeth I loved to go hunting. Here she is **hawking** (see page 9) with her **courtiers**.

Tudor Life

ENTERTAINMENT

Nicola Barber

WAYLAND

First published in 2009 by Wayland

Copyright © Wayland 2009

Wayland
338 Euston Road
London NW1 3BH

Wayland Australia
Level 17/207 Kent Street
Sydney NSW 2000

Senior Editor: Claire Shanahan
Designer: Jane Hawkins
Picture Researcher: Kathy Lockley

British Library Cataloguing in Publication Data
Barber, Nicola
Entertainment. - (Tudor life)
1. Amusements - Great Britain - History - 16th century -
Juvenile literature 2. Popular culture - England - History
16th century - Juvenile literature 3. England - Social
life and customs - 16th century - Juvenile literature
I. Title
790'.0942'09031

ISBN 978 0 7502 5756 5

Picture acknowledgements Art Archive: 12,
Art Archive/British Library: 16, 28B, Art Archive/
Museo Civico Cremona/Gianni Dagli Orti:
COVER (Main), 7, Bibliotheque Nationale,
Paris, France/Lauros/Giraudon/Bridgeman Art
Library, London: 22, Bridgeman Art Library/
Getty Images: 21, Mary Evans Picture Library:
20, Mary Evans Picture Library/Alamy: 8, 10, 17,
Helmingham Hall, Suffolk, UK/Mark Fiennes/
Bridgeman Art Library: COVER (Inset), 24, 28T,
Museum of London: 5, 11, North Wind Archives/
Alamy: titlepage, 25, Parham Park, Nr Pulborough,
West Sussex, UK/Bridgeman Art Library, London: 4, 19, Andrea Pistolesi/Getty Images: 23, The Print
Collector/Alamy: 6, 18, Private Collection, Abbott & Holder, London, UK/Bridgeman Art Library, London: 27,
Private Collection/Photo © Christie's Images/Bridgeman Art Library, London: 14, Private Collection/© Philip
Mould Ltd, London/Bridgeman Art Library, London: 13, Scottish National Portrait Gallery, Edinburgh,
Scotland/Bridgeman Art Library, London: 26, TopFoto/Fotomas. TopFoto.co.uk: 9, Victoria & Albert Museum,
London/Bridgeman Art Library, London: 15

Printed in China

Wayland is a division of Hachette Children's Books, an Hachette UK company.
www.hachettelivre.co.uk

Tudor life

The vast majority of the population in Tudor times lived in small villages in the countryside. London was the biggest city, with a population of more than 250,000 by 1600. Other notable towns and cities included Bristol, Norwich and York.

Tudor society was divided into different social classes. The **monarch** was the most powerful person in the land. The monarch's **royal court** was made up of members of the nobility and senior religious figures. Ordinary people ranged from wealthy merchants and businessmen to the poorest **peasants**. The Tudors passed many laws to control the lives of the ordinary people – including the kinds of entertainment that were allowed.

A game often played around Easter time was the egg dance. The performer had to complete the dance without crushing the egg.

Written at the time

As well as being a passionate sportsman, Henry VIII loved poetry and music. He wrote this poem and set it to music:

'Pastime with good company,
I love, and shall until I die.
Grudge who likes, but none deny,
So God be pleased, thus live will I.
For my pastance:
Hunt, sing, and dance,
My heart is set!
All goodly sport,
For my comfort,
Who shall me let?'

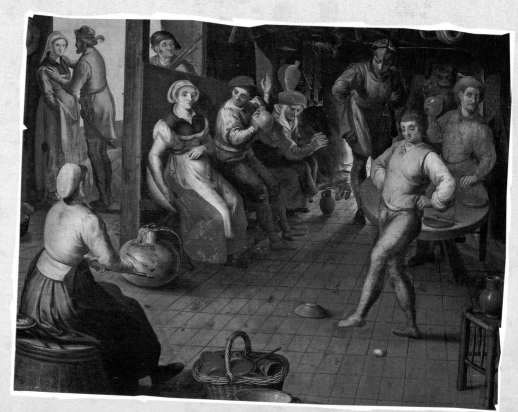

Pastimes for the rich

For royalty and the nobility during Tudor times, there was a wide range of pastimes. **Jousting**, hunting, **real tennis**, chess and card games were all popular.

A joust of 1510 featuring Henry VIII and an opponent. You can see the king's **lance** shattering as he scores a direct hit.

Jousting tournaments

Tournaments were like mock battles. They started in the twelfth century, and were originally intended as training for real battles. By Tudor times, jousting was the central part of a tournament. Two armoured horsemen charged towards each other on either side of a barrier, called the tilt. Both horsemen held long wooden lances with which they tried to unseat each other. Jousting was dangerous – splinters from shattered lances could cause injury, as could falling from a galloping horse. Many nobles had special heavy armour that they wore just for jousting.

Hunting

Henry VIII and Elizabeth I loved to hunt, and they both spent many hours on horseback in pursuit of deer. After a hunt, the meat from the deer was eaten.

Written at the time

In 1524, Henry VIII was injured during a jousting accident when he failed to close the visor (the hinged part that is pulled forward to protect the face) on his helmet during a joust with the Duke of Suffolk:

'Then the duke set forward and charged with his spear, and the king likewise unadvisedly set off towards the duke. The people, seeing the king's face bare, cried hold, hold; the duke neither saw nor heard, and whether the king remembered his visor was up or not few could tell. Alas, what sorrow was it to the people when they saw the splinters of [the] duke's spear strike the king's headpiece.'

During the mid-winter when deer hunting stopped, the monarch and nobles went hawking with falcons and hawks. These birds were trained to hunt small birds and animals.

Real tennis

Real tennis is a type of tennis that is played on a special indoor court (lawn tennis developed from real tennis in the 1800s). Henry VIII loved the game so much that he had a court built at Hampton Court, which is still in use today. The king played with a wooden racquet and balls made from leather that were stuffed with rags or horsehair.

⬆ Real tennis is played on an enclosed court that has sloping roofs, called penthouses, on three sides.

Feasts

The Tudors held feasts to celebrate festivals such as Christmas. Tudor monarchs and nobles also used feasts to display their wealth and power.

⬆ Henry VII at a royal banquet in 1508. Two serving boys bring food to the table.

Christmas feasts

The main feast of the year for both rich and poor was Christmas. Christmas celebrations started on Christmas Day itself, 25 December, and lasted for 12 days, ending on Twelfth Night (3 January). For wealthy families, the centrepiece of their Christmas feast was a **boar's** head, presented with an apple or lemon in its mouth and crowned with holly, ivy and rosemary.

A Tudor object

This jug is made from black leather. It has a lid that is attached to the handle with a metal hinge. The leather was made waterproof by treating the skin side with beeswax, or with the sap from a birch tree, which was boiled and rubbed into the leather. Jugs such as this one were used to hold water or other drinks. The liquid was poured into smaller leather tankards for drinking.

During the Tudor period, leather jugs such as this were known as Bombards because they were a similar shape to the barrel of a type of gun called a bombard.

Christmas treats

Henry VIII was one of the first people in England to eat turkey for his Christmas feast. This bird was brought to Europe by the Spanish, and the first turkeys appeared in England in the 1520s. Only royalty and the nobility could afford to eat it. The less well-off ate **mutton** or pork at Christmas.

Mince pies had a filling made from 13 ingredients, including fruit, dried fruit and spices, to represent Jesus Christ and his 12 **apostles**. People ate one mince pie every day for the 12 days of Christmas to bring good luck for the 12 months ahead.

Food to impress

Wealthy Tudors ate a great deal of meat and fish – vegetables were considered more suitable for ordinary people. Fruit was a luxury, particularly exotic fruits such as peaches and apricots that were either imported from abroad or grown specially.

Lavish feasts were laid on when important people came to visit. These feasts had many courses, with meat in spicy sauces, pies and pastries, and elaborate decorations made from sugar.

Masques

Music, dance, poetry and drama were combined in events called masques for wealthy Tudors. They were usually performed at festivals, or celebrations such as Christmas or weddings.

Lavish spectacles

Masques were performed at the houses of the rich, often outside during the summer months. No expense was spared in creating spectacular costumes and elaborate wigs. All the people that took part in a masque wore masks over their faces to disguise their identities. Often, the wealthy **patrons** themselves took part – including women. King Henry VIII loved to act in his own masques, and the first recorded appearance in court of Anne Boleyn, who went on to become Henry's second wife, was on 1 March 1522, when she took part in a masque.

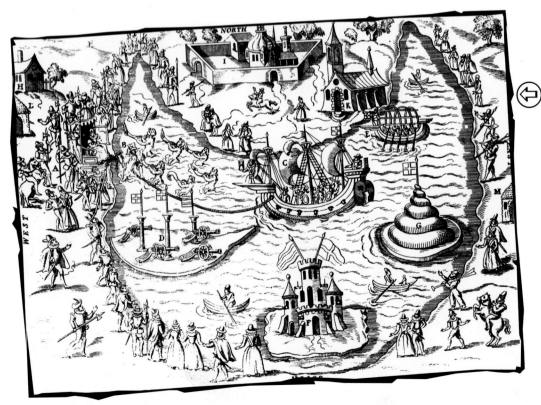

This engraving shows a masque that was organised by the Earl of Hertford for Elizabeth I in 1591. The entertainment took place on a miniature lake.

Some of the leading poets, **dramatists** and musicians of the day wrote the words and music for masques. They included Edmund Spenser, Francis Beaumont and John Fletcher, and the composers William Byrd and Thomas Campion.

Royal progressions

Like her father, Elizabeth I loved masques, although she rarely took part. Every summer, Elizabeth and the members of her court set off on a royal progression around the country. This was a way for the queen to show herself to her people. Elizabeth stayed in her own palaces and houses, and in the houses of her nobles, who vied with each other to put on lavish entertainments for their queen.

In 1575, the queen visited her favourite courtier, Robert Dudley, at his house in Kenilworth. Dudley himself starred in the masque that was written for the occasion.

Edmund Spenser, 1552/3–99

The poet Edmund Spenser came from a poor family. He was educated at the Merchant Taylors' School in London, and at Cambridge University. In the 1570s, he went to Ireland to work for the English governor and, for his part in putting down a rebellion, he was awarded land there. His best-known poem is 'The Faerie Queene', which was dedicated to Elizabeth I and published in the 1590s. On his death in 1599, he was buried with great ceremony in Westminster Abbey.

This portrait, which dates from the 1590s, is said to be of the poet Edmund Spenser.

Holy days and festivals

Holy days and festivals were times of celebration for both rich and poor. The festivities on these days included feasts (see pages 10–11), entertainments, tournaments and other sporting events.

Holy days

Holy days were days that were set aside by the Church. On these days, people were forbidden to work and they had to go to church. Holy days included Christmas, Epiphany (6 January), Ascension Day (the fifth Thursday after Easter) and All Saints (1 November). After attending church, most people celebrated with a feast.

May Day

May Day was an important spring festival. A queen of the May was chosen from the girls in each village, and there was dancing around a maypole – often with each dancer holding one of the ribbons that was attached to the top of the pole.

This painting by the Dutch painter Pieter Brueghel the Younger shows a May Day dance around the maypole.

Accession Day

During the reign of Elizabeth I, the day that Elizabeth became queen, 17 November, was celebrated every year as Accession Day. This day became a major festival both at court and across the country. Every year, there was an elaborate court entertainment with jousting and poetry, which the public could attend. In every town and village, people lit bonfires, rang the church bells, and held feasts.

This portrait shows Richard Sackville, Earl of Dorset wearing his Accession Day clothes in 1616 for the celebrations of Elizabeth I's successor, James I.

Written at the time

A German traveller called Lupold von Webel described the Accession Day entertainment at court in 1584:

'About twelve o'clock the queen and her ladies placed themselves at the windows in a long room at Weithol [Whitehall] palace, near Westminster, opposite the barrier where the tournament was to be held ... Round the barrier stands were arranged ... so that everybody by paying 12d. would get a stand and see the play ... Many thousand spectators ... got places, not to speak of those who were within the barrier and paid nothing.'

Favourite pastimes

In Tudor times, there were laws to govern which sports ordinary people could play. These laws were relaxed at Christmas to allow people to enjoy themselves.

Games and sports

Popular pastimes included games of dice and cards, board games, bowls and skittles. But in 1512, Henry VIII passed a law to ban people from playing almost all games and sports, except archery. Henry wanted people to be fit for work, and he needed good archers for his army.

This illustration in a manuscript from 1500 shows men playing shinty.

Football became popular in the early 1500s, although it was not like the game that we know today. The goalposts were often a mile apart, and there was no limit to the number of people on a team. Whole villages challenged each other, and most games ended with several serious injuries. Henry VIII tried to ban football completely in 1540. Other team sports included stoolball (an early type of cricket), rounders, and hurling or shinty (similar to hockey).

Philip Stubbs wrote with great disapproval in *The Anatomy of Abuses* in 1585 about the dangers of football:

'Football is more a fight than a game... Sometimes their necks are broken, sometimes their backs, sometimes their legs... Football encourages envy and hatred... sometimes fighting, murder and a great loss of blood.'

Fighting and baiting

Some of the most popular spectator sports were cockfighting and bull- and bear-baiting. Such 'bloodsports' are illegal today, but these violent forms of entertainment were popular with both the rich and poor in Tudor times. Queen Elizabeth I loved to attend these shows.

There were special baiting rings in most towns and cities, where up to 1,000 people could watch. Both bulls and bears were tied to posts and then attacked by dogs. Cockerels fought each other in a cockpit, battling with their beaks and feet until one of them was killed. People loved to gamble on the outcome of these bloody contests.

 Bear-baiting was one of the cruel sports that were extremely popular in Tudor times.

Children's pastimes

Children in Tudor times did not have to go to school, and many children from poor families began work at a young age. Most children had few toys and they had to entertain themselves in their spare time.

Games and toys

Some of the games that were played by Tudor children are still around today, including blind-man's bluff, hopscotch and marbles. Wealthy parents could afford to buy wooden toys, such as dolls and toy ships, which were beautifully carved and painted. Other favourite toys included **popguns**, kites, drums and hobbyhorses. Trumpets were made from cows' horns, and simple pipes from plant stalks. Old barrels were used to make wooden hoops, and pigs' **bladders** were blown up to make footballs.

⬇ Several children's toys and games are shown here: from left to right, a rattle, a windmil, a hobbyhorse, two children playing catch and a boy blowing soap bubbles with a reed.

Outdoor life

Children from wealthy families learned how to ride and to hunt from a young age. Many poor children also spent a lot of time outdoors, fishing or playing in local streams or rivers. It was common to see children amongst the crowds that watched the gruesome spectacles of animal baiting and cockfighting (see pages 16–17), as well as public executions (see pages 26–27). Children also loved the shows put on by the bands of actors who travelled from town to town (see pages 20–21).

Boy bishops

St Nicholas is the patron saint of children. On St Nicholas' Day, 6 December, it was the custom to choose a boy to act as bishop until the Feast of the Holy Innocents (28 December). This honour was often given to the youngest choirboy, who was dressed in a small bishop's costume and often took services in the cathedral or church. This practice was **abolished** by Elizabeth I, but it still continues in some English cathedrals to this day.

A Tudor object

From a young age, girls were taught to fill any spare time with needlework. They practised on pieces of work called samplers until they became skilled at the many different embroidery stitches. Embroidery was used to decorate a wide range of items from clothes to furnishings. Many girls also learned to make exquisite lace. This piece of embroidery (below) is thought to be the work of Queen Elizabeth I.

⬆ This embroidered cloth shows a scene from Greek mythology, as Actaeon (right) disturbs the goddess Diana as she bathes (centre).

Travelling actors

In Tudor times actors, musicians and entertainers, often called 'strolling players', travelled from one place to another. They performed in market squares or in the courtyards of inns.

A play is performed on a temporary stage in the courtyard of an inn.

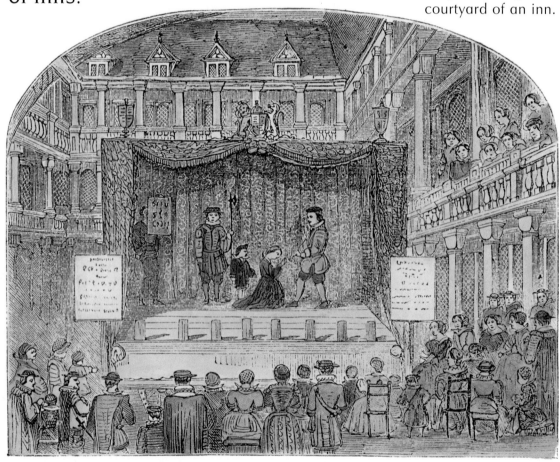

Beggars and vagabonds

Although many people enjoyed the entertainments put on by these strolling players, others treated them with great suspicion. People who travelled from place to place to earn a living were often considered to be beggars or **vagabonds**. Many people believed that the strolling players could spread diseases like the **plague** from place to place.

In 1572, the government of Elizabeth I passed a law to force all strolling players to belong to an official 'company' with the backing of a noble patron. Many of these companies were known by the names of their patrons, for example the Earl of Pembroke's Men, and the Earl of Leicester's Men. After 1576, when the first permanent theatre was set up (see pages 22–23), many of these companies began to perform in theatres, rather than inn courtyards or marketplaces.

Boys' companies

The companies of strolling players were all men – women were not permitted to take part in such entertainments. Men or boys played all the women's parts. There were also two companies of boys, the Children of the Chapel Royal at Windsor and the Boys of St Paul's Cathedral. Both of these companies performed for Henry VIII and Elizabeth I on special occasions. They also gave private performances for members of the nobility.

This engraving of William Shakespeare was published in the *First Folio* (the first printed and collected edition of Shakespeare's plays) in 1623.

William Shakespeare, 1564–1616

William Shakespeare was born in Stratford-upon-Avon in Warwickshire, and went to the grammar school there. He married when he was 18 years old. In 1594, he became a member of the Lord Chamberlain's Men. He quickly became the main dramatist for the company, as well as acting on stage. The company performed at the Globe Theatre on the south bank of the River Thames in London. Today, Shakespeare is the most famous of all the Tudor dramatists, and his plays are performed all over the world.

Theatres

The first permanent public theatre was established in 1576 by the actor James Burbage, and was called simply the Theatre. It was in Shoreditch, north of the city of London.

London theatres

Soon, other theatres were being built around London, including the Rose (1587), the Swan (1596) and the Globe (1599). All of these theatres were on the south bank of the River Thames. Different companies performed at different theatres, and competed with each other to pull in the biggest audiences.

This sketch shows a scene from Shakespeare's play *Titus Andronicus*. It was probably drawn in 1594 by an actor called Henry Peacham.

The Globe

The most successful of all the theatres was the Globe, as this was where the Lord Chamberlain's Men were based, and their main dramatist was William Shakespeare (see page 21). The original Globe theatre burned down in 1613 when a cannon that was shot during a performance of Shakespeare's *Henry* VIII accidentally set light to the thatched roof.

Written at the time

A visitor from Switzerland, named Thomas Platter, described a performance of Shakespeare's play *Julius Caesar* at the Globe theatre in 1599:

'On September 21st after lunch, about two o'clock, I and my party crossed the water, and there in the house with the thatched roof witnessed an excellent performance of the tragedy of the first Emperor Julius Caesar with a cast of some fifteen people; when the play was over, they danced very marvellously and gracefully together as is their wont, two dressed as men and two as women.'

The Globe was rebuilt to an even grander design, but was pulled down in 1644. Today, the Globe has been rebuilt once more, and you can experience Shakespeare's plays just as a Tudor audience would have done.

Theatre design

The Globe and other Elizabethan theatres were circular in shape. On the inside, a gallery with a thatched roof ran around the edge, and a roof covered the raised stage, which jutted out into the middle. In front of the stage was a yard or 'pit' where people crowded in to watch the plays. Audiences were often rowdy and noisy, particularly the 'groundlings' who stood in the pit.

⇧ Shakespeare's plays are still performed at the Globe today.

Music and dance

Music and dance were very popular forms of entertainment in Tudor times, both at court and among the ordinary people.

Music at court

For Tudor kings and queens and their courtiers, learning to play and to perform music was considered an important skill. Henry VIII was a talented musician, and is said to have composed the famous tune for the song 'Greensleeves'. Elizabeth I was a skilled performer on the lute (a plucked instrument held like a guitar), and the virginals (a type of harpsichord). During this period, music for groups of instruments, called **consorts**, became popular. Composers such as William Byrd and John Dowland wrote for consorts of viols (stringed instruments that were held between the knees), and recorders of different sizes.

Country and church

Away from the refined tastes at court, ordinary people sang folk songs and **ballads**, and played instruments such as the bagpipes, and a loud woodwind instrument called the shawm. Music was also an important part of church services, particularly in the country's cathedrals, where choirs of men and boys sung music that was written by composers such as Thomas Tallis and William Byrd.

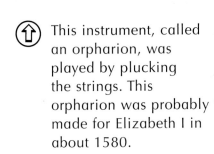

⬆ This instrument, called an orpharion, was played by plucking the strings. This orpharion was probably made for Elizabeth I in about 1580.

Dance

Dancing was very popular with both rich and poor, but the types of dance performed at court and elsewhere were quite different. Many court dances came from France, Spain or Italy. Dance masters were employed to teach both royalty and the courtiers these elaborate dances, which had names such as the pavane, galliard and the volta.

Ordinary people danced at celebrations such as May Day (see page 14). On these occasions, everyone joined in country dances such as jigs, and the men performed Morris dances – some with heavy sticks that they would clash together in time to the music.

Thomas Tallis, c.1510–1585

Little is known about Thomas Tallis's early years, but during his long life he wrote music for all the Tudor monarchs. He became a Gentleman of the Chapel Royal in 1543, where he performed and composed music for Henry VIII. He is probably best known for his **motet** 'Spem in alium', which is written for eight five-part choirs – 40 voices! It was possibly written for the 40th birthday of Elizabeth I in 1573.

Dancing was a popular pastime in Tudor England.

Public executions

In Tudor times, public executions were a popular form of entertainment. People queued to get the best places, and executions often had a carnival atmosphere.

Harsh justice

Tudor justice was very harsh. People could be sentenced to death for many different crimes, including **treason**, murder, rebellion against the government or even minor crimes such as stealing food.

The kind of execution depended on a person's social class. Members of royalty or the nobility were usually beheaded. After beheadings, the heads of the criminals were sometimes stuck on spikes in public places as reminders to everyone of the dangers of breaking the law. For ordinary people, executions included hanging, being burned to death, or even being boiled alive.

The execution of Mary Queen of Scots in 1587. Accounts of the execution tell that it took two blows of the axe to cut off her head completely.

A private execution

One of the most famous executions held in Tudor times was that of Anne Boleyn after she was convicted of treason in 1536. Because it often took several blows of the axe to cut the head off the body, Henry sent for a swordsman from France to perform the execution. The swordsman cut through Anne's neck with one expert blow. Although the execution of Anne Boleyn was not a public event, it was nevertheless watched by several hundred noblemen and women, all members of Henry's court.

⬆ Burning at the stake was a terrible form of death often used to punish treason or heresy (challenging accepted religious beliefs).

The Tyburn Tree

Common criminals convicted in London were usually executed in Tyburn, where Marble Arch stands today. In Tudor times, Tyburn was a village in the countryside outside London. In 1571, a large **gallows** was built there, called the Tyburn Tree. Several criminals could be hanged at once, so Tyburn was often used for mass executions, which attracted huge crowds.

Written at the time

During his visit to England, Thomas Platter observed an execution at Tyburn:

'... when the trial is over, those condemned to the rope are placed on a cart, each one with a rope about his neck, and the hangman drives with them out of the town to the gallows, called Tyburn, almost an hour away from the city; there he fastens them up one after another by the rope and drives the cart off under the gallows... '

Timeline

1485	Battle of Bosworth Field and death of Richard III. Beginning of the Tudor era when Henry VII becomes king.
1492	Christopher Columbus sails to the Americas.
1509	Death of Henry VII; Henry VIII succeeds to the throne and marries Catherine of Aragon.
1533	Henry VIII marries Anne Boleyn.
1536	Death of Catherine of Aragon; execution of Anne Boleyn; Henry VIII marries Jane Seymour.
1536–40	Henry VIII closes down the monasteries in England.
1537	Birth of Prince Edward (later Edward VI); death of Jane Seymour.
1540	Henry VIII marries and divorces Anne of Cleves; marries Catherine Howard.
1547	Death of Henry VIII; Edward VI succeeds to the throne.
1553	Death of Edward VI; Lady Jane Grey becomes queen for nine days; Mary I succeeds to the throne.
1554	Mary I marries King Philip II of Spain.
1558	Mary I dies; Elizabeth I succeeds to the throne.
1568	Mary Queen of Scots flees to England.
1576	First permanent public theatre established, called the Theatre.
1587	Execution of Mary Queen of Scots.
1587	Rose theatre built.
1588	Defeat of the Spanish Armada.
1596	Swan theatre built.
1599	Globe theatre built.
1603	Death of Elizabeth I. End of the Tudor era.

Glossary

abolish to do away with, or put an end to something

apostle one of the twelve disciples of Jesus Christ

ballad a song (or poem) that tells a story

bladder the organ in a human or an animal's body where urine is stored

boar a male wild pig

consort in music, a consort is the name for a group of instruments such as viols or recorders, and the music written for such a group

courtier a member of the royal court

dramatist a person who writes plays (drama)

gallows the frame on which criminals were hanged

hawking hunting with falcons and hawks. These birds were trained to hunt small birds and animals

joust a competition between two armoured horsemen who charged towards each other holding long wooden lances with which they tried to unseat each other

lance a long wooden spear

monarch a ruling king or queen

motet a piece of music for many different parts, often for voices

mutton the meat of an adult sheep

patron someone who pays for and supports artists, musicians or writers

peasant a poor person who works on the land

plague a very infectious disease that is passed to people by the bites of infected fleas

popgun a toy gun

Protestant describes the churches that separated from the Roman Catholic Church in the sixteenth century

real tennis a type of tennis that is played on a special indoor court. Lawn tennis (the tennis that we play today) developed from real tennis

reign the period of a time that a king or queen serves as a monarch

Roman Catholic Church the Christian church that is governed by the pope, from the Vatican City in Rome

royal court the household that is centred on a king or queen

tournament in Tudor times, a series of mock battles that were staged for entertainment. The centrepiece of a tournament was usually jousting

treason the crime of betraying your country, for example by helping your country's enemies

vagabond someone who has no permanent home or job, and who travels from place to place

Index

Resources

People in the Past: Tudor Rich and Poor Haydn Middleton, Heinemann 2003

History in Art: Tudor England Nicola Barber, Raintree, 2005

Your Tudor Homework Helper Alice Proctor, Ticktock, 2005

Eyewitness Guides: Tudor Simon Adams, Dorling Kindersley 2008

http://www.nettlesworth.durham.sch.uk/time/tudors.html
The site of Nettlesworth Primary School has lots of fun information about the Tudors.

http://www.tudorhistory.org/
Links to lots of information about the Tudors.

http://www.headlinehistory.co.uk/index.htm
Online history site.